You Can't Go Back

I0809155

You Can't Go Back

Shirley Coleman

Acclaim Press
MORLEY, MISSOURI

Acclaim Press
— Your Next Great Book —
P.O. Box 238
Morley, Missouri 63767
(573) 472-9800
www.acclaimpress.com

Book design: Chelsea Steele
Cover design: M. Frene Melton.

Coleman, Shirley.
You can't go back / by Shirley Coleman.
p. cm.
ISBN-13: 978-1-935001-71-3 (alk. paper)
ISBN-10: 1-935001-71-X (alk. paper)
1. Regret--Religious aspects--Christianity. 2. Consolation. I. Title.
BV4909.C64 2011
248.8'6--dc22

2011013835

First Printing 2011
Printed in the United States of America
10 9 8 7 6 5 4 3 2 1

Dedication

To my husband, Dewayne,
for his support and love,
which helped me finish the dream
of writing this book.

Contents

The Journey

Writing a book is like trying to plan out your whole life, and you're only beginning life. So many times we stop and we think, "If only I could go back and change things… if only I could go back I would not make the same mistakes," but we can't go back. Life moves forward, and so must we.

We learn out best lessons in life from the mistakes we make. We can apologize for harsh words, things we break, promises we didn't keep, but we can't go back… when we fail to kiss someone we love and we see them no more... we fail to say the words in our heart because we think that maybe next time, we fail to touch or hug someone special because we think maybe later. Later sometimes never comes. To the child who wanted only a few seconds of their parents' time to talk, and on the way to school the child was killed in a car accident. To the father who wanted only a few seconds to talk to his teenage son and tell him, "I am sorry," but that never made it out of the house because his heart failed.

Remember it is the journey, not just the destination that carries meaning and fulfillment.

You Can't Go Back

The Dream

I woke up in a hospital; started asking the doctors' questions, and they started asking questions. It all started… then I began to tell about my life before the incident.

One day I had all I could take, so I went for a walk in the woods. Don't know what happened; I remembered I had to choose what road to take. The one road was all grown up with weeds, as though there had been no one down that path in a long time. The other road was well paved and looked as though many had chosen this path. I sat on a stump that was near the road looking and wondering which direction I might go. I finally decided that it really didn't matter which road I would take, because if one didn't work out all I had to do was go back. Little did I know that there was no going back.

So being down and out I decided to take the road less traveled. I felt at this time I needed to be alone. The less people I had to see the better. My life was a total mess and so was I. I felt the past year of my life had finally caused the walls to close in on me. All I wanted to do now was to run as far away from my problems as I could.

Who I Am Makes a Difference

You may have read this story already, but I felt it was worth reading again.

A teacher in New York decided to honor each of her seniors in high school by telling them the difference they each made. She called each student to the front of the class, one at a time. First she told each of them how they had made a difference to her and the class. Then she presented each of them with a blue ribbon imprinted with gold letters, which read, "Who I Am Makes a Difference."

Afterwards the teacher decided to do a class project to see what kind of impact recognition would have on a community. She gave each of the students three more ribbons and instructed them to go out and spread this acknowledgment ceremony. Then they were to follow up on the results, see who honored whom and report back to the class in about a week.

One of the boys in the class went to a junior executive in a nearby company and honored him for helping him with his career planning. He gave him a blue ribbon and put it on his shirt. Then he gave him two extra ribbons and said, "We're doing a class project on recognition, and we'd like you to go out, find somebody to honor, give them a blue ribbon, then give them the extra blue ribbon so they can acknowledge a third person to keep this acknowledgment ceremony going. Then please report back to me and tell me what happened."

Later that day this junior executive went in to see his boss, who had been noted by the way, as being kind of a grouchy fellow. He sat his boss down and told him that he deeply admired him for being a creative genius. The boss seemed very surprised. The junior executive asked him if he would accept the gift of the blue ribbon and would he give him permission to put it on him. His surprised boss said, "Well, sure." The junior executive took the blue ribbon and placed it right on his boss's jacket above his heart. As he gave him the last extra ribbon, he said, "Would you do me a favor? Would you take this extra ribbon and pass it on by honoring somebody else? The young boy who first gave me the ribbons is doing a project in school and we want to keep this recognition ceremony going and find out how it affects people."

That night the boss came home to his 14-year-old son and sat him down. He said, "The most incredible thing happened to me today. I was in my office and one of the junior executives came in and told me he admired me and gave me a blue ribbon for being a creative genius. Imagine. He thinks I'm a creative genius. Then he gave me this ribbon and asked me to find somebody else to honor. As I was driving home tonight, I started thinking about whom I would honor with this ribbon and I thought about you. I want to honor you. My days are really hectic and when I come home I don't pay a lot of attention to you. Sometimes I scream at you for not getting good enough grades in school and for your bedroom being a mess, but somehow tonight, I just wanted to sit here and, well, just let you know that you are the most important person in my life. You're a great kid and I love you!"

The startled boy started to sob and sob, and he couldn't stop crying. His whole body shook. He looked up at his father and said through his tears, "Dad, earlier tonight I sat in my room and wrote a letter to you and Mom explaining why I had killed myself and asking you to forgive me. I was going to commit suicide tonight after you were asleep. I just didn't think that you cared at all. The letter is upstairs. I don't think I need it after all."

His father walked upstairs and found a heartfelt letter full of anguish and pain. The envelope was addressed, "Mom and Dad."

The boss went back to work a changed man. He was no longer a grouch and made sure to let all his employees know that they made a difference. The junior executive helped several other young people with career planning and never forgot to let them know that they had made a difference in his life… one being the boss's son. And the young boy and his classmates learned a valuable lesson.

Who you are DOES make a difference. You never know what kind of difference a little encouragement can make to a person. Who you are makes a difference, and I wanted you to know that!

This was a letter I received from a dear friend.

> I was regretting the past and fearing the future.
>
> Suddenly my Lord was speaking, "My name is I Am…"
>
> He paused, I waited.
>
> He continued, "When you live in the past with it mistakes and regrets it is hard. I am not there.
>
> "My name is not I was. When you live in the future, with its problems and fears, it is hard. I am not there.
>
> "My name is not I will be. When you live in the moment it is not hard, I am here.
>
> "My name is I AM."
>
> —*Helen Mallicoat*

You Can't Go Back

The day has just begun; the sun is slowly rising above the hill. The air is crisp and fresh as it gently blows through the clean, white curtains. Christmas is almost here and all is well. As I lie here and contemplate my day's journey I think of the dream and it's meaning, not knowing quite how to start.

Thoughts of _____ keep entering my mind; should I call, should I write or should I check on her? This question plagued me 30 years ago and I did nothing. Now I have the guilt and pain to live with. I think maybe I will take the change and if I make a fool of myself for calling then a fool I will be, but at least I will not be making the same mistakes twice.

There is one thing in life we can't do and that is to go back. So many times in life after we have reached a certain point in our life, we wish we could go back and say or do something that we should have done before, but one thing for certain we can't go back. If we could go back, I would turn back my clock some 50 years or so, to my childhood where growing up in a rural community with numerous siblings, meant never a quiet moment.

Since I can't go back in reality, I will go back in memory where events and circumstances of my life can be brought to the surface so you can better understand the dream.

Family

On December 7th, 1949, a little blue-eyed girl was born in the unusual county of Miner, MO, population some 100 or so, the eleventh child of a soon to be family of twelve. The young girl, Sunshine, remained the baby of the family for four years until a new sister arrived. The little blue-eyed girl born on Pearl Harbor day was soon to be the child that endured the blunt end of all of her brothers' practical jokes. A few years later the new baby arrived. Number twelve was now the baby and very protected. Shortly after her arrival, eleven days, a brother was killed and the joy of her birth was saddened by the loss of her 19-year-old brother. The story was that a man who mysteriously ran over Donnie. He was on his way home from work at McDonald Douglas in St. Louis, MO, when the accident occurred. He was riding his motorcycle when the car came up from behind and hit him, throwing him over the bridge. He died shortly after the accident, with a broken neck and internal injuries. The driver was never found, although they had a description of the car and part of the license number.

Donnie was married with a beautiful daughter and awaiting the birth of his son when his life was taken.

One child was born on June 13, and another taken on June 24. Sadness loomed over the house the next few months. The gifted child of the family was gone. His young life ended before he could ever see his son, who was born on December 7th the same day as the eleventh child of the family. Shortly after the grandson's birth, two days, Donnie Jr., his mother, and his mother's sister had a wreck coming home from the hospital. The sister died, the mother was seriously injured, and remained in the hospital for a long time. The new baby and his sister went to live with the grandparents. Now there were an additional two children in the family, two babies only six months apart, one a daughter, the other a grandson. The grandson over the next few years was raised with the family as a brother instead of a nephew. The niece went back home with the mother after she was released from the hospital.

During this time Sunshine was watching and observing all those she loved, trying her best to make everyone laugh, even when she had to be the blunt end of her brothers' tricks. You see, her brothers were continuously trying to make her cry or sad so she wouldn't be so bright and sunny. You may think it was jealously that made them do this, but actually it was just their way of showing they cared, because they knew that Sunshine would always come up smiling.

Don't Judge Life By One Season

A Story I Was Told:

There was a man who had four sons. He wanted his sons to do things too quickly. So he sent them each on a quest, to reach a pear tree that was a great distance away.

The first son went in the winter. The second in the spring, the third in the summer, and the youngest son in the fall. When they had all gone and come back, he called them to tell what they had seen.

The first son said that the tree was ugly and bent, and the second son said, no, it was covered with green buds and full of pears, sweet, and looked so beautiful. The third son disagreed; he said it was laden with blues and purples and was the most graceful. The last son disagreed with all of them: he said it was covered with fruit, full of life and fulfillment.

The man then explained to his sons that they were all right, but each had seen but only one season in the tree's life.

He told them that you cannot judge a tree, or a person, and that the essence of who they are and the pleasure from that life can only be measured at the end.

If you give up when it is winter, you will miss the beauty of your summer, prosperous of your spring, and fulfillment of your fall.

Moral:

Don't let the pain of one season destroy the joy of another.

Don't judge life by one difficult season.

Persevere through the difficult patches and better times are sure to come sometime or later.

Sunshine

You may be wondering how Sunshine got her name. Well, when she was born the old doctor that delivered her at home said she came into the world with the most delightful laughter he had ever heard and that her eyes were as bright as the sunshine. Over the years to come the old doctor and Sunshine become friends. The old doctor told the father that this was the child that would bring him the greatest joy of all. The little girl grew up to be a Daddy's daughter and the apple of his eye as the doctor had told him. Everything the daddy did, Sunshine was right beside him, very interested and very understanding. She loved her father very much. So you can see the brothers didn't hate Sunshine, they just knew that she would do and accept things they would not. Over the years to come they would reflect on these times.

Hunting

The father loved to go hunting, but the boys found it too much work to walk so far in the snow, to hunt just a rabbit or two. They didn't stop to think that they were missing the best time of their lives, the quality time of being with their father, and having the precious time without any interruptions to find out what type of man he was or the sweet little stories of wisdom he would tell. Those stories were told with love and with a purpose, that the father thought Sunshine would never know he was speaking of her. The stories were always about someone else that the father had known.

The first adventure Sunshine was allowed to take with her father and to go hunting was something she would never forget.

The boys were complaining it was too cold and they didn't feel good. So father told them okay, he would go alone, but Sunshine begged that she would be good and not complain if he would let her go. He finally said okay, if she would bundle up good. He said that Sunshine could carry the rabbits back home that they caught. She was so proud to get to go that in her haste she forgot the cold and only put on one pair of socks under her boots. The day was bitterly cold. Strong winds, and falling snow only made things worse. It seems as though they walked for miles, before returning home. Each step that father took, Sunshine was right behind stepping into the huge tracks that he had made. Her little feet getting colder by the minute, but the cold was worth it just to have the time to be with father, and to see that smile and hear those stories. After each story he would turn around and smile and say, "Everything okay?" Sunshine would smile and answer, "Yes." Although she was freezing, the warmth of the smile seemed to be worth the small amount of pain that the cold was placing upon her. Finally, after a successful day they went home. Soon as they got home father and Sunshine cleaned the rabbits and then went to get out of their wet clothes, and to get some hot chocolate. Sunshine headed straight for the old coal stove to get warm. Father was coming with the hot chocolate and she still hadn't removed her boots. He had sat her down, so he could take off the boots. She knew that he would find out about the socks and she would never get to go hunting again. She was scared.

The tears ran down her cheeks as daddy removed her boots. He looked up at her with those stern, but gentle, blue eyes, and then looked at her feet. He grew quiet as he had mother bring some towels so he could bring back the circulation in Sunshine's feet and warm then slowly, so there would be no damage. It seemed like a lifetime before he said a word. He spoke in his quiet voice, but he didn't yell or lecture. He began to tell her a story of a young boy who loved his friend so much that he sacrificed all he had to give his friends a few moments of happiness. It was at this time she knew how important her father was to her. She thought she had seen a tear flow down his cheek, but he said, "It was just the cold in my eyes." You see this was a time and era when men were not to show their affection or feelings, because it was not manly to cry. But she knew his feelings because words didn't have to be said to know how she felt or how he felt. They both just seemed to know and feel what the other was thinking.

Her feet eventually thawed and she finally got warm, but that day was a special day for her and if she had to freeze to death she would have still been warm from the gentle smile.

The next morning, bright and early, Sunshine heard her father in the kitchen cooking the rabbits they had caught for breakfast. When everyone came to breakfast her chest was out as far as it could go over the proud task of being part of providing that morning's breakfast. The boys in their usual manner were making sly comments about the rabbit.

"This rabbit is all bruised. What happened, pep squeak. Couldn't you carry the rabbit? Did you have to drag it and bruise it all up?" and "Remember, she doesn't have enough sense to put on the right amount of socks. How can you expect her to know how to carry a rabbit?" "Don't give her such a hard time…." She thought for a moment one brother had some kindness then she heard, "We're lucky she didn't stop father from shooting them, and try to get him to bring them home for pets, you know how she is about saving all those poor helpless creatures." Although their comments were sad, she kept smiling and thinking, "Poor dumb brothers, they don't even know what they missed." She looked at her father and saw the glow in his eyes and then the wink, and knew that he was thinking the same thing.

The Pearls

The cheerful little girl with the bouncy, golden curls was almost five. Waiting with her mother at the checkout stand, she saw them, a circle of glistening, white pearls in a pink, foil box. "Oh mommy please, Mommy. Can I have them? Please, Mommy, please?" Quickly the mother checked the back of the little box and then looked back into the pleading, blue eyes of her little girl's face. "A dollar ninety-five; that's almost $2.00. If you really want them, I'll think of some extra chores for you. In no time you can save enough money to buy them for yourself. Your birthday's only a week away and you might get another crisp dollar bill from Grandma."

As soon as Jenny got home, she emptied her penny bank and counted out 17 pennies. After dinner, she did more than her share of chores and she went to the neighbors and asked Mrs. McJames if she could pick dandelions for ten cents. On her birthday, Grandma did give her another new dollar bill and at last she had enough money to buy the necklace.

Jenny loved her pearls. They made her feel dressed up and grown up. She wore them everywhere, Sunday school, kindergarten, even to bed. The only time she took them off was when she went swimming or had a bubble bath. Mother said if they got wet, they might turn her neck green.

Jenny had a very loving daddy and every night when she was ready for bed, he would stop whatever he was doing and come upstairs to read her a story. One night as he finished the story, he asked Jenny, "Do you love me?"

"Oh yes, Daddy. You know that I love you."

"Then give me your pearls."

"Oh Daddy, not my pearls. But you can have Princess, the white horse from my collection, the one with the pink tail. Remember Daddy? The one you gave me. She's my very favorite."

"That's okay Honey, Daddy loves you. Goodnight." And he brushed her cheek with a kiss.

About a week later, after the story time, Jenny's daddy asked again, "Do you love me?"

"Daddy, you know I love you."

"Then give me your pearls."

"Oh Daddy, not my pearls. But you can have my baby doll. The brand new one I got for my birthday. She is beautiful you can have the yellow blanket that matches her sleeper."

"That's okay, sleep well. God bless you, little one. Daddy loves you." And as always, he brushed her cheek with a gentle kiss.

A few nights later when her daddy came in, Jenny was sitting on her bed with her legs crossed Indian style. As he came close, he noticed her chin was trembling and one silent tear rolled down her cheek. "What is it, Jenny? What's the matter?"

Jenny didn't say anything but lifted her little hand up to her daddy. And when she opened it, there was her little pearl necklace. With a little quiver, she finally said, "Here, Daddy, this is for you." With tears gathering in his own eyes, Jenny's daddy reached out with one had to take the dime store necklace, and with the other hand he reached into his pocket and pulled out a blue velvet case with a strand of genuine pearls and gave then to Jenny. He had them all the time. He was just waiting for her to give up the dime-store stuff so he could give her the genuine treasure. So it is, with our Heavenly Father. He is waiting for us to give up things in our lives so that he can give us beautiful treasures.

Jenny learned God will never take away something without giving you something better in its place. The greatest gifts happen when you share love and touch others.

Cotton Pickin'

Being a country family and living in a small community meant that everyone knew everyone, and meant a lot of hard work. The boys, being their usual lazy selves, worked hard at getting out of work. In the summer when it was cotton pickin' time the boys were their usual mean selves. Sunshine, being too young to pick enough cotton to matter, was used by her brothers to weigh in as cotton. They thought how nice it would be to get paid for a few extra pounds of Sunshine.

They decided to tie her hands and gag her mouth so she couldn't yell and she was placed in their cotton sack with all of their cotton. She was weighted and dumped, but to their surprise they weren't the ones that got to dump the cotton sack that day. Father was at the top of the wagon. Though they begged and pleaded that they would be glad to dump the sacks, father told them that was okay, he would do it.

It being very unusual that they were so eager to help, father knew something was up. He was expecting bricks or dirt clots in their sacks, but even he was shocked when Sunshine was dumped out from the sack. Gasping for breath and crying when untied and ungaged she was so relieved. She thought this was the ultimate stunt and her end. She need not say a lot about what happened to her brothers.

Father was never one to raise his voice; he had no need to. You just knew that when he spoke he meant it. The boys were exceedingly quiet for a few weeks and sitting was something they didn't do for sometime either. The panic of her father's eyes was something not easily forgotten. I think that stunt was one the boys aren't likely to forget either. Sunshine had experienced darkness and fear that she had never felt before. She was so grateful to be in her father's arms and to know she would be safe. The warmth of knowing someone cared meant something special. To a child being protected in this way meant that no matter what happened someone special was there and everything would be okay.

The Storm

The sirens were going off and we knew there was a storm coming. As usual, Mother and Daddy gathered up all the kids, we were headed off to the Doziers' storm cellar. Everyone in the community, all 46, decided we needed a shelter during storms and tornados. Everyone got together and dug this huge hole and we buried an old bus in the hole.

The wind was starting to blow hard, and hail was coming down; we were all running as fast as we could to make it to the shelter. The boys as usual were mumbling and laughing, acting like macho men taking their good old time. Finally we made it; it felt so good in the shelter with our kerosene lamps, old quilts, and snacks. The little ones were all quiet, listening to the adults tell stories about storms they had heard about, and fantasies about things they had seen and endured, all the time laughing and teasing each other. It was a good time where for a moment we enjoyed the fellowship of each other. Some laughs, some tears. Everyone felt safe in that old bus. No fears of what was going on outside just the joys of what was going on inside. The time passed quickly and soon the storm was over and it was time for everyone to go home, and see what damage was done. The children all ran out first, then Gene and Gene, a couple of young men helped everyone else out of the bus. On one occasion Noke, the owner of the land and my best friend's father, got stuck trying to get out of the bus. He was a large man and Gene and Gene pulled till they finally got him out. Next was Eula Grigsby, a tiny, elderly lady who always wore black and lived alone by the old graveyard. A lot of the kids in the community thought she was a witch because of her clothes and the fact that she lived all alone.

After struggling to get Noke out of the bus, when they grabbed Eula, they pulled harder than they had wanted and she went soaring threw the air. The kids all said, "Look, she is a witch, she's flying through the air!" Needless to say, everyone that said a word about her being a witch got into a lot of trouble. Sometime later we all discovered what a nice, lonely lady she was, but that night we had the chance to enjoy life, to laugh, to cry, and time to discover what true friendship, and to be grateful we all survived the storm.

Lady in Black

In the community where Sunshine lived there were a few elderly people who needed a lot of caring for. There was one lady in particular whom the children in the community thought was a witch. She lived behind the graveyard in an old shanty house. She had no indoor plumbing, so her water had to be drawn from a well out back, for drinking, bathing, and other uses.

She always wore black. The kids all thought this was a true sign of her being a witch, along with her black cat she kept in the house. All of the kids had to pass her house on the way to the fishing hole.

She would sit on the porch in her rocker with her cat on her lap as the kids passed by. One day on the way to the fishing hole Sunshine, being a curious child, decided to talk to the lady in black. She knew that even if she went on to the fishing hole all her brothers would let her do would be to carry the worms for their fishing pleasures. So today she decided to ignore her brothers, and discover who the lady in black was and if she was a witch, Sunshine would have to take her chances. Running ahead of the other kids, she laid the worms down on the path ahead of them and ran upon the porch to talk to the lady. The other kids were telling her she was going to get in trouble and the witch would put a spell upon her, and she would never be the same again. The boys were mad because she had laid the worms down and they would not have anyone to do their work for them. Sunshine did have a spell put on her, but not by a witch, but by a warm, loving, lonely widow who was full of wisdom and generosity. Sunshine and the lonely widow soon became very good friends.

Sunshine enjoyed going to her house in the evenings, and pumping water, and visiting with her. Her father told her that the lady had lived there for over forty years, and had only one son whom lived in another state, and only came to see her when he was able. Her husband had died shortly before Sunshine was born, so the lady lived a quiet life alone in the house where her husband and she lived. After his death she decided to stay put instead of going with her son to his home.

Over the years she mourned and dressed in black because of her love for her husband, and because she loved black. She enjoyed watching the children go by, even though she knew they were afraid of her. Sunshine soon learned that the lady was full of love and happiness, and soon the other kids learned this too.

After a short while it became a natural habit of stopping at the shanty, little house, and helping with the little chores Eula needed and enjoying the treats she would make for all the kids. Going fishing soon meant more than just fishing. It was more like an adventure to see what was in store for the kids next. Eula soon became friends with all the kids in the neighborhood. What the kids learned that summer was that the lady they thought was a witch, was not, and that by sharing their time and love they received the greatest gift of all, the mystery of the old and the adventure and love in giving to someone in need.

As the years went by Eula's health slowly went down and one quiet summer night she left this world for a better world to be with her husband. Sunshine was thirteen at the time and one thing she learned from the lady was the gift of sharing your love and how special this was, to give your all for those you love.

Shortly after this her home was torn down and a business put in its place. Somehow the old path to the fishing hole was never the same again. But memories will always be there and the thoughts of that first step in discovering the mystery of the lady in black. Also, this was one of the first times Sunshine disobeyed her brothers and went out on her own.

What Goes Around Comes Around

One day a woman was walking down the street when she spied a beggar sitting on the corner. The man was elderly, unshaven and ragged. As he sat there, pedestrians walked by him giving him dirty looks. They clearly wanted nothing to do with him because of who he was—a dirty, homeless, man. But when she saw him, the woman was moved to compassion.

It was very cold that day and the man had his tattered coat—more like an old suit coat rather than a warm coat—wrapped around him. She stopped and looked down. "Sir?" she asked. "Are you all right?"

The man slowly looked up. This was a woman clearly accustomed to the finer things in life. Her coat was new. She looked like she had never missed a meal in her life. His first thought was that she wanted to make fun of him, like so many others had done before. "Leave me alone," he growled.

To his amazement, the woman continued standing. She was smiling—her even white teeth displayed in dazzling rows. "Are you hungry?" she asked.

"No," he answered sarcastically. "I've just come from dining with the president. Now go away."

The woman's smile became even broader. Suddenly the man felt a gentle hand under his arm. "What are you doing, lady?"

the man asked angrily. "I said to leave me alone."

Just then a policeman came up. "Is there any problem, ma'am?" he asked.

"No problem here, officer," the woman answered. "I'm just trying to get this man to his feet. Will you help me?"

The officer scratched his head. "That's old Jack. He's been a fixture around here for a couple of years. What do you want with him?"

"See that cafeteria over there?" she asked. "I'm going to get him something to eat and get him out of the cold for awhile."

"Are you crazy, lady?" the homeless man resisted. "I don't want to go in there!" Then he felt strong hands grab his other arm and lift him up. "Let me go, officer. I didn't do anything."

"This is a good deal for you, Jack," the officer answered. "Don't blow it."

Finally, with some difficulty, the woman and the police officer got Jack into the cafeteria and sat him at a table in a remote corner. It was the middle of the morning, so most of the breakfast crowd had already left and the lunch bunch had not yet arrived. The manager strode across the cafeteria and stood by the table. "What's going on here officer?" he asked. "What is all this. Is this man in trouble?"

"This lady brought this man here to be fed," the policeman answered.

"Not in here!" the manager replied angrily. "Having a person like that here is bad for business."

Old Jack smiled a toothless grin. "See, lady. I told you so. Now if you'll let me go. I didn't want to come here in the first place."

The woman turned to the cafeteria manager and smiled, "Sir, are you familiar with Eddy and Associates, the banking firm down the street?"

"Of course I am," the manager answered impatiently. "They hold their weekly meetings in one of my banquet rooms."

"And do you make a goodly amount of money providing food at these weekly meetings?"

"What business is that of yours?"

"I, sir, am Penelope Eddy, president and CEO of the company."

"Oh."

The woman smiled again. "I thought that might make a difference." She glanced at the cop who was busy stifling a giggle. "Would you like to join us in a cup of coffee and a meal, officer?"

"No thanks, ma'am," the officer replied. "I'm on duty."

"Then perhaps, a cup of coffee to go?"

"Yes ma'am. That would be very nice."

The cafeteria manager turned on his heal, "I'll get your coffee for you right away, officer."

The officer watched him walk away. "You certainly put him in is place," he said.

"That was not my intent. Believe it or not, I have a reason for all this." She sat down at the table across from her amazed dinner guest. She stared at him intently. "Jack, do you remember me?"

Old Jack searched her face with his old, rheumy eyes. "I think so—I mean you look familiar."

"I'm a little older perhaps," she said. "Maybe I've even filled out more than in my younger days when you worked here, and I came through that very door, cold and hungry.

"I was just out of college," the woman began. "I had come to the city looking for a job, but I couldn't find anything. Finally I was down to my last few cents and had been kicked out of my apartment. I walked the streets for days. It was February and I was cold and nearly starving. I saw this place and walked in on the off chance that I could get something to eat.

Jack lit up with a smile. "Now I remember," he said. "I was behind the serving counter. You came up and asked me if you could work for something to eat. I said that it was against company policy."

"I know," the woman continued. "Then you made me the biggest roast beef sandwich that I had ever seen, gave me a cup of coffee, and told me to go over to a corner table and enjoy it. I was afraid that you would get into trouble. Then, when I looked over, I saw you put the price of my food in the cash register. I knew then that everything would be all right."

"So you started your own business?" Old Jack said.

"I got a job that very afternoon. I worked my way up. Eventually I started my own business that with the help of God, prospered." She opened her purse and pulled out a business card. "When you are finished here, I want you to pay a visit to a Mr. Lyons. He's the personnel director of my company. I'll go talk to him now and I'm certain he'll find something for you to do around the office." She smiled, "I think he might even find the funds to give you a little advance so that you can buy some clothes and get a place to live until you get on your feet. And if you ever need anything, my door is always opened to you."

There were tears in the old man's eyes. "How can I ever thank you?" he said.

"Don't thank me," the woman answered. "To God goes the glory. Thank Jesus. He led me to you."

Outside the cafeteria, the officer and the woman paused at the entrance before going their separate ways. "Thank you for all of your help, officer," she said.

"On the contrary, Ms. Eddy," he answered. "Thank you. I saw a miracle today, something that I will never forget. And thank you for the coffee."

She frowned. "I forgot to ask you whether you used cream or sugar. That's black."

The officer looked at the steaming cup of coffee in his hands. "Yes, I do take cream and sugar—perhaps more sugar than is good for me." He patted his ample stomach.

"I'm sorry," she said.

"I don't need it now," he replied smiling. "I've got the feeling that this coffee you bought me is going to taste as sweet as sugar."

Swinging Bridge

Sometimes in life we stop and think, "If only I had done something different," or we think about the past and wonder, "Why didn't I call my friend more?" or "Why didn't I write a letter to my sister when she was sick?"

I often think of a dream I had years ago about the swinging bridge. In the dream, I saw a friend crossing the bridge and another friend on the other side, safe and secure. It was time for me to cross the bridge but I was scared, so I decided not the cross the bridge but to find another way to get to the other side. A few minutes later the bridge broke and my friend went into the water. She did not survive the fall. Shortly after, I awoke and could not forget the dream. Later in my life I lost a brother who died on a bridge.

After the dream, I learned to start enjoying my life and realized that I had been given another shot at living. I also learned to seize every minute of every day.

Angels have no need for faith; faith is what sustains us.

"Now I lay me down to sleep,
I pray the Lord my soul to keep."

When I awake in the morning I will see the sun in all its glory. Reoccurring—the swinging bridge.

But faith is the strongest sister of them all. Hope is frail and fragile. Charity has love and compassion.

We were meant to act even if we make a mistake; that is why we put a sharp point on the pencil and why we put on eraser on the other end.

> Hebrew 11:1: *For with faith all can be accomplished. It is the substance of things hoped for and the evidence of things not seen.*

Faith shall set you free; better to have all of faith for a while than the price of it forever. When two people are on a journey, there are times when they will fall in love. That doesn't mean they have to go on separate journeys. "I can't find myself back to the Lord." Stand up and walk.

Prisoner of Probability.

Dreams are the roots to another world. Death is a miracle, a soul passing from one sphere to another.

Clean up unfinished businesses before you leave. Prayers are always answered, sometimes the answer is no, sometimes the answer is not yet, and sometimes the answer is yes.

Marie

Sunshine's brothers were constantly telling her she was an orphan and belonged to an old mean looking insurance man that came by the house to collect insurance. Sunshine knew that this was a lie, because she knew she could only belong to her father, although, once they almost convinced her different, because of her hair, complexion, blue eyes, and blond hair, which was a trait only she had, not the other children. Father was blue-eyed, but had dark hair and a dark complexion, and mother had dark hair and green eyes. Grandfather, my father's father, was an Indian, most of the children developed his traits, where as Sunshine got her blond hair and blue eyes from her grandmother.

This fact didn't help her because of her differences from the other children. Sunshine's older sister, Marie, didn't like this either. Mother would dress the two children alike and Marie, the oldest, not wanting this, rebelled. She was always making alterations in her clothes before getting on the bus. You see, Marie was a twin and her twin died when they were babies, so mother somehow tried to replace the twin with Sunshine who was just a couple of years younger.

Marie, being a twin and a runt, seemed to always get her way with mother because she was so small and fragile, or at least mother and a few others thought so. Marie was indeed petite, but very powerful, just like dynamite. She was upset with Sunshine because she caught up with her in the 4th grade and now that both Marie and Sunshine were in the same grade, she felt people would really think they were twins. You might think this was funny if you had seen the two together, one pale face, blond hair, blue eyes, and very quiet and patient, the other short, loud, hot tempered, with dark auburn hair, and green eyes. Marie was determined she was going to be as good as any boy, and tomboy she was. She got into more trouble than a pack of wolves in the hen house, with the farmer standing shotgun over them.

Tornado

There was the time when Marie and Sunshine were in the 6th grade, and a tornado hit the old homestead. By God's grace no one was hurt, except one mean brother who was hit in the head with something when he tried to open the front door. But as you can imagine, this was not serious because there wasn't much that could be damaged when one had little upstairs anyway.

The house was destroyed and there was the matter of what to do with eleven kids. At this time there was a cousin, a niece, and a nephew living there. The children were all distributed among the neighbors. Sunshine and Marie went together to a neighbor that had no children of her own. The couple wanted children, but could not have them. So, the two girls were treated like little princesses for the next couple of months. Sunshine loved this because she loved the pretty starched dresses and white pinafores, but Marie was outraged, she wanted her old pants and to do her own thing.

Manners, she protested, parties, she detested, and being showed off, she despised. She did show her respect and tried to do her best to mind the couple who cared for her, but this took all the willpower she could muster up. She also knew that if she didn't listen, Father would find out and then she would be in trouble. One thing Father always taught was to respect your neighbors and friends. This was one thing all of the children knew well. It wasn't long until the garage was built, and petitions were put up to act as room dividers, and everyone could return and live as a family until the new home was completed. Marie was on cloud nine the day she discovered this. She thought, "Now I can go back to wearing my pants, and no more stiff dresses and ribbons."

Life soon returned to normal, or back to the way it was, which was not normal. The boys returned to being their mean selves, Marie happy to be back and out of the dresses, and the babies were glad to see everyone. The family was now all back home. For awhile all the kids seemed to appreciate things better, and even once the boys were civilized to Sunshine and the other sisters in the house. Once, Marie was even caught trying one of the dresses on and admiring herself in the mirror. I guess something good can come from something bad. A few months later the new home was completed, and along with the new home came indoor plumbing, and a telephone, and a television. This being a first for all of the family, there was great excitement in the house.

The Light in the Window

The time spent living in the garage was also a significant time for Sunshine. This was the start of her strange dreams. One night while sleeping with Marie and Ann she had this terrible fear come upon her, she felt as though she was awake but she knew she was sleeping. She had seen a light pass by her bedroom window and the light kept returning. Earlier that day she heard an elderly neighbor telling some people about a lamp man that worked for the railroad and how he had slipped and fell about the time the train started to move. It was said that the man's head was never found and at night you could still see the light from the lantern where the man searched for his head.

That night while sleeping Sunshine thought the man was passing her window. She was so scared she couldn't even scream. She laid there for what seemed like hours trying to move, and trying to wake one of her sisters, or to even speak so she could scream for help, but nothing worked. Then she started praying and finally something in her moved and she went straight for her father in the next room.

And straight is where she went too, because to leave the room you had to go a ways and go around a sheetrock petition. She took the shortcut and went straight through the sheetrock and jumped into bed with mother and father.

Safe again in her father's arms she knew everything would be okay. Soon she realized that she had a bad dream, but that fear stayed with her for a long time.

The boys found this very amusing, so once again Sunshine became the blunt end of their jokes. At night you would hear them yell out to each other, "Did you make sure the doors are all open and everything is out of Sunshine's way, you know how she loves leaping through the walls." Then there would be the harmony of voices yelling, "Sunshine, you better watch out, he thinks that you know where his head is." Then Father would tell them that was enough and it was time for sleep. That episode took a long time before it was forgotten or set aside for a better event.

Snipe Hunting

One of the boys' favorite stories, which were told throughout the years, was the day they took Sunshine snipe hunting. Sunshine very much loved the outdoors and hunting, so to get to go snipe hunting was something special. For one thing her brothers were going to actually take her with them, and for another thing, she had never seen a snipe and didn't have any idea what it was. But being happy about going, she decided not to make waves and ask, she figured they would tell her soon enough.

So with her sack and stick in hand, she was off into the woods or might I say graveyard that was in the woods. She was given instructions to sit upon an old stump with the sack open and to watch and wait. They, the boys, said you had to be real quiet and the snipe would come up and go right into the sack and if he didn't go all the way in you are to hit him with the stick then close the sack and tell and they would come and get him. You see, each person was to find a different position away from everyone so the snipe wouldn't get scared and run away.

Still not knowing what this creature looked like, Sunshine was assured that she would know it when she found it.

So off the boys went and there Sunshine sat waiting for her snipe. She didn't mind, it was a pleasant fall day and the sun was shining bright. But soon the sun disappeared and no boys or snipe. It was starting to get a little cool and Sunshine started hearing strange noises. Once she knew it wasn't a familiar voice and she knew that dead people couldn't talk, or so she thought.

Fear finally sat in and she began to cry. She was getting cold and hungry, and her imagination was running wild. Had the snipes devoured her brothers, or were they hurt or lost, she didn't know. All she knew for sure was that she was in the middle of a graveyard with a sack and stick, sitting on a stump and she was scared and all alone.

Back at the house, Father had started looking for Sunshine and couldn't find her anywhere. It was past suppertime and none of the neighbors had seen her for hours. None of the girls knew where she was; Marie told Father the last time she had seen Sunshine was when the boys took her snipe hunting.

Marie, not knowing what a snipe was either, became scared when Father asked her again where Sunshine was. Marie told him the boys had taken her into the woods to look for snipe and that she didn't want to go because she wasn't feeling well, so she stayed home. Marie asked Father if he thought a snipe might of got her. Father told her not to worry, he knew the creatures that knew her whereabouts.

It wasn't long until father found the boys and they took him to where Sunshine was. With flashlight in hand, Father went into the dark, damp graveyard. Sunshine, by this time, had cried so much that all she had left in her was a fragile whimper. She saw the light approaching and didn't know if this was a friend or foe. She bowed her tiny little head and began to pray.

All at once she felt these safe warm arms around her and knew immediately without even opening her eyes, this was Daddy. He wrapped his jacket around her and lifted her in his arms and took her home where she would be safe again. Through tears and whispers she told her father that she had failed, because she hadn't caught a snipe and because she was not brave enough to not cry. She told him that she was scared and was afraid that something had happened to the boys and that when it got dark she just didn't know what to do. Father in his usual soft voice held her close and told her not to worry, because he knew she hadn't failed. He assured her the boys were all right, at present that is. Safe at home Sunshine ate her supper, dressed and went to bed.

Marie came in and gave Sunshine a big hug, and told her she was glad a mean snipe hadn't eaten her. Soon Father came in and Marie and Sunshine asked Father what a snipe was. Father began to laugh and then told the girls the story about snipe, and his first time snipe hunting. Soon they were all laughing and everything felt good, except for the boys in the other room. For some reason they weren't laughing.

This was a day Marie was glad she had stayed at home. As for Sunshine, it was an adventure not much different than others the brothers placed her in. Father, that night, told the girls a story about a young boy who thought he had failed in life because he had tried so hard to be brave, and to do what he was told by his mother, but because he couldn't accomplish the task the way he thought she wanted it done he felt that he had failed her.

Later the boy's mother asked him what was wrong and told her how he couldn't get the tree she had wanted, but only another similar to it. The mother told the son he had done well even though he had not been able to get the one she sent him for. He tried and got one similar to the one she wanted and in doing so, he brought back a tree even more worthy than she had expected. He tried and that was the main thing, he could have just as easily came home with nothing and explained the tree she wanted was gone, but instead he made a decision and tried to succeed at his task. This, the mother said was what makes the tree much better than any other, because it was specially chosen by him.

This story, like so many others Father told, was sending a message. A message of love and the message that it is not so much that we fail in our task as if it is that we fail to try to succeed.

Once again Father's voice and story eased the heart of one little scared Sunshine. All was well now, safe at home in bed with Marie and Ann. Tonight even Marie was laughing and happy. I think she was even scared of Sunshine, even though she would never admit it. That night Marie talked nonstop and held on to Sunshine like she held on to her favorite pillow, still clinging to her the next morning.

Though we are indeed human and not much different from our fellow humans, we all fail at certain tasks in our lives, it is when we stop trying and give up that failure takes over, but as long as we keep trying, even if we do fail, we can learn from these failures and become stronger and better for having tried.

Children in Darkness

The key to success is education. In the world today for so many children this key seems like an impossible dream. These children are living in homes where there are drugs, abuse, filth, and vast other complications, no food, no heat, no lights, and the list goes on. So many children live in darkness, they are afraid to tell others what is happening to them. It may be because of a fear that someone will hurt someone they love, or ashamed and guilt for what has been done to them. They live in, no they exist in, a world of darkness, trying to pretend it is all a nightmare and someday they will awake. For these children it seems there is no light at the end of the tunnel.

Sometimes in life we don't want to enjoy love because we don't want to hurt. In life we all have dreams of becoming something important and doing great things, but because we often become afraid of failing, we never try or take the chance.

Too often the person afraid of giving themselves and take chances on life itself fails, and the soul who fears death as new beginning becomes afraid of living life to the fullest and enjoying each day of life they have, they exist instead of living.

Others say love is a razor that leaves you alone to bleed, love is not easy when someone we love hurts, we hurt, when they feel pain, we feel pain, when they die we feel as though someone took a razor and ripped our heart until it bleeds.

Love is a hunger, and an endless need. We need someone to care for us, to be there for us as we need food to keep us from being hungry and keep us from feeling empty inside. But I say love is a flower and you need its only seed. If the nsight has been too lonely, and the road has been too long. Remember, things in life sometimes take us down paths that may seem endless, and we feel as though we are never going to make it to our destination and that we are all alone, and no one is beside us as we travel down the lonely road.

We begin to think love is only for the lucky and the strong, for those who are willing to take chances, suffer the hurt and laughter, the good times and the bad, and do what it takes to endure the traits of love. Always remember in the winter, the cold, harsh, bitter trials of life and love, far beneath the filter lie, the need, the beginning of life that is planted deep in the ground all the bitterness of the coldness, that with the sun's warmth that true love begins, and in the spring, the time of new beginning and growth. The seed that had been planted becomes a rose.

For each seed of love that you plant in the heart and the soul of someone else the beauty of the rose can be seen in all its glory. Remember, love isn't easy, but its beauty can be enjoyed. God loved the world that he gave his only begotten son, so that you can be spared.

If we don't plant the seeds the rose cannot grow. If we don't plant the seed of love then life will lose all the beauty we enjoy each day. The laughter of a child, the little things someone cares about, or a quiet place to sleep.

There is not a soul on this entire Earth that doesn't have a burden to carry; you are not alone with that. But remember, you have carried this burden long enough it is time to lay down and go on. Sometimes we think we don't know how, but remember you have a choice. Either start or stop. It's time for you to come out of the shadows and choose. You may think you can't, but God says yes you can, you are not alone, and I am here with you. I have been here with you all along. Yesterday is the past; tomorrow is the future. Today is a gift—that's why it's called the present.

The rose is known for providing sweet fragrance, just as an angel is known for providing sweet peace.

> Ephesians 2:8-9: *For by grace you have been saved though faith; and that not of yourselves, it is the gift of God; not of works, lest any man should boast.*

> Ephesians 4:32: *And be ye kind to one another, tender-hearted, forgiving one another, even as God for Christ's sake has forgiven you.*

> 2 Corinthians 4:18: *While we look not at the things which are seen, but at the things which are not seen: for the things which are seen are temporal; but the things which are not seen are eternal.*

Love the seed, that with the sun's love, God's love, in the spring becomes the rose in all its beauty, the gift that we give, the gift of peace, and love. Love is like a flower and you its only seed. If we don't plant the seeds of love and kindness, then love cannot be shown. In the Bible Samuel says: "…for man looketh on the outward appearance, but the Lord looketh on the heart."

Rose

Growing up: a very graceful experience.

The first day of school, our professor introduced himself and challenged us to get to know someone we didn't already know. I stood up to look around when a gentle hand touched my shoulder. I turned around to find a wrinkled, little old lady beaming up at me with a smile that lit up her entire being. She said, "Hi handsome. My name is Rose. I'm eighty-seven years old. Can I give you a hug?"

I laughed and enthusiastically responded, "Of course you may!" and she gave me a giant squeeze.

"Why are you in college at such a young, innocent age?" I asked.

She jokingly replied, "I'm here to meet a rich husband, get married, have a couple of children, and then retire and travel."

"No seriously," I asked. I was curious what may have motivated her to be taking on this challenge at her age.

"I've always dreamed of getting a college education, and now I'm getting one!" she told me.

After class we walked to the student union building and shared a chocolate milkshake. We became instant friends. Every day for the next three months we would leave class together and talk nonstop. I was always mesmerized listening to this "time machine" as she shared her wisdom and experience with me. Over the course of the year, Rose became a campus icon and she easily made friends wherever she went. She loved to dress up and she reveled in the attention bestowed upon her from the other students. She was living it up.

At the end of the semester we invited Rose to speak at our football banquet. I'll never forget what she taught us. She was introduced, and stepped up to the podium. As she began to deliver her prepared speech, she dropped her three by five cards on the floor. Frustrated and a little embarrassed, she leaned into the microphone and simply said, "I'm sorry I'm so jittery. I gave up beer for lent and this whiskey is killing me! I'll never get my speech back in order, so let me just tell you what I know."

As we laughed, she cleared her throat and began: "We do not stop playing because we are old; we grow old because we stop playing. There are only four secrets to staying young, being happy and achieving success. You have to laugh and find humor every day. You've got to have a dream. When you lose your dreams, you die. We have so many people walking around who are dead and don't even know it! There is a huge difference between growing older and growing up. If you are nineteen years old and lie in bed for one full year and don't do one productive thing, you will turn twenty years old. If I am eighty-seven years old and stay in bed for a year and never do anything I will turn eighty-eight. Anybody can grow older. That doesn't take any talent or ability. The idea is to grow up by always finding the opportunity in change. Have no regrets. The elderly usually don't have regrets for what we did, but rather for things we did not do. The only people who fear death are those with regrets."

She concluded her speech by courageously singing, "The Rose." She challenged each of us to study the lyrics and live them out in our daily lives. At the years-end Rose finished the college degree she had begun all those years ago. One week after graduation, Rose died peacefully in her sleep. Over two thousand college students attended her funeral in tribute to the wonderful woman who taught by example that it's never too late to be all you can possibly be. Remember, growing older is mandatory, growing up is optional.

In loving memory of Rose.

Thanksgiving

Thanksgiving was approaching and work had to be done. The boys, knowing this, always seemed to have excuses or good explanations to return from any work that the holidays might have placed upon them. Their favorite excuse and trick was the mysterious sickness that caused a slight fever, nausea and severe headaches, and sometimes the ever-convincing rash.

This particular Thanksgiving brought new surprises for the boys. While preparing the big picture as to who was to be the sickest and who was going to be the caretaker of the poor misfortunate boys, they made one big mistake.

You see, Sunshine had actually been sick just a few days before, and they couldn't play any of their tricks on her, so they thought they would try their hand of trickery on Marie. Well, this is where they made their first goof-up. For as I said earlier, Marie was very protected by mother because of her size and the fact that she was the surviving twin. Marie knew Mother would listen and believe anything she said. She used her size and misfortune very well to get what she wanted. She was the mischievous one that knew what she wanted, and how to get it.

The boys forgot about Marie's strong advantage over them, and forgetting that unlike Sunshine, who usually said nothing and went along with their tactics, Marie was one that sought vengeance on those who dared cross her path. Marie thought she was as though and as strong as the boys, and in many ways she was even stronger.

Unfortunately, the boys earlier in the week had taken Marie and hung her on a hook in the barn for a couple of hours before she was discovered. Like I said, she was one to seek vengeance, and vengeance she sought. She lurched up and peeked around every corner watching every move the boys made, waiting for the right moment and time, and here it was.

The boys were discussing the master plan and Marie with her mean mind, knew that all she had to do was the devise her own plan and make the boys pay for their cruelty. The boys had decided that the rash would be needed this time, so they could have a couple of days extra to rest and special treatment when it came to Thanksgiving dinner. They knew mother would baby them and fix their plates and have the girls to wait on them until their rash went away.

You see, they had conjured up a potion of powder, baking soda and other ingredients I will not name because of a family secret, to produce this magnificent rash that lasted two to three days.

Meanwhile, Marie was waiting for the nighttime to in act her plan. Marie went through the house that day smiling and whistling the best she could, knowing that soon it would be her time to get even with the boys. She was so happy that she even told Mother that she would be glad to go to the store and get the things mother needed for the day. Sunshine, still recuperating from her illness, was in total shock over Marie's reply.

For you see, Marie had one thing in common with the boys, she hated work as much, if not more, than they did.

Ann and Sunshine usually took the walk to the little country store about a mile down the road. Marie was usually too fragile to go, but today Marie declared to Mother that she would be delighted to go with Ann to the store. She felt fresh air would do her good, and besides she told Mother she had some money saved up, and there was something she wanted to buy to make Sunshine smile and feel better again. Mother was so delighted in Marie's change that she never even asked what Marie had bought for Sunshine. It was a good thing that she didn't, or Marie's sweet, innocent demure that she showed Mother would have been discovered. By now you are probably wondering what the gift was and what in the world had Marie planned for the boys.

It was the morning before Thanksgiving, and the boys, waking early, had devised their plan and place the potion all over themselves. Each helping the other to rub it in and make sure they had an even rash. "Don't want to make Mother suspect anything," David said.

The girls were also awake in the other room, quietly listening to the boys laughing over how they were so smart and how those dumb girls would have to wait on them hand and foot. The girls were also laughing quietly waiting for Marie's plan to work.

Soon the boys crawled back in bed and covered up head-to-toe so no one would be the wiser and know that they had already been up. The girls, also not wanting to be discovered, followed the lead.

Soon mother was yelling, telling everyone it was time to get up. The boys started their moaning routine, followed by mother entering and enquiring what was wrong. Soon Edward proceeded to run out, pretending to be nauseated, followed by David's complaining, "I think I have a fever."

The next step was the rash. Needless to say, Mother soon yelled at the girls to bring the lotion for the boys to help soothe their itchy rash. Edward had so convincingly produced tears and complained he was itching so bad that it hurt all over.

Marie, in her sweet voice, said she would gladly rub Edward's back to help relieve the horrible itching. You see, Edward was the one that hung Marie on the hook.

All smiles and kindness, the girls started rubbing the boys with the lotion, while Mother proceeded to the kitchen with Ann to start breakfast, which the boys knew that they would get in bed and the girls would bring it to them. Marie was so kind to Edward while rubbing the lotion on him that frozen butter would have melted in her mouth.

Edward was somewhat scared of Marie's actions, knowing that she never agreed to do anything without a fight, and to be pleasant and smiling, he was terrified. He knew all too well her past history, and he was now remembering the event that occurred a few days before. It wasn't long before the girls were through and went to wash their hands, and to help mother prepare breakfast for the boys.

Marie's first plan had already taken place and now part two of the plan was to take effect. Soon breakfast was brought to the boys and as usual they complained they didn't know if they could eat or not, but they would try. Marie told them she had brought each one of them something special that would make them feel better.

Ann was a good hand at baking, and she and Marie had convinced Mother to let them prepare the boys some hot muffins to go along with breakfast. Since they were sick, they should be given special attention.

Marie told Edward since he was the sickest; Ann and she had prepared him a special muffin with extra blueberries and chocolate pieces. This was Edwards's favorite. All went well and plan two was now in effect. The girls retrieved the dirty dishes and were in the kitchen cleaning up when it happened.

David started yelling, "Mother come quick, something's

wrong!" Terrified, yet knowing, the boy's mother went to investigate. The rash was no longer a rash. The boys were swelling and blotches began to appear all over them. Dean was crying, "he really was itching and it hurt like hell!" Soon Edward became deathly sick, puking his guts out crying "this is not supposed to happen! What went wrong?" Between the sickness, itching and misery they began arguing among themselves.

"Did you add the wrong stuff in this? We're always sure to measure correctly" Soon Mother was back in the room, but not until she had overheard part of their conversation.

That Thanksgiving the boys learned what it meant to be thankful and how to give. For the next month they gave and gave and gave until they were thankful for their time of punishment to be over. They also learned not to mess with Marie.

You see, dynamite does come in small packages, and is very explosive, and dangerous to your health. The boys learned this well.

White Lie Cake

A story from a friend.

Have you ever told a white lie? You are going to love this…especially all of the ladies who bake for church events.

Alice Grayson was to bake a cake for the Baptist Church ladies' group bake sale in Tuscaloosa, but she forgot to do it until the last minute. She remembered it the morning of the bake sale and after rummaging through cabinets she found and angel food cake mix and quickly made it while drying her hair, dressing and helping her son Bryan pack up for Scout camp. But when Alice took the cake from the oven, the center had dropped flat and the cake was horribly disfigured. She said, "Oh dear, there's no time to bake another cake." This cake was so important to Alice, because she did so want to fit in at her new church and in her new community of new friends. So, being inventive, she looked around the house to build up the center of the cake. Alice found it in the bathroom—a roll of toilet paper. She plunked it in and then covered it with icing. Not only did the finished product look beautiful, it looked perfect!

Before she left the house to drop the cake by the church and head for work, Alice woke her daughter Amanda and gave her some money and specific instructions to be at the bake sale the minute it opened at 9:30 a.m. and to buy that cake and bring it home. When the daughter arrived at the sale, she found that the attractive perfect cake had already been sold. Amanda grabbed her cell phone and called her mom.

Alice was horrified. She was beside herself. Everyone would know, what would they think? "Oh, my," she wailed! She would be ostracized, talked about, ridiculed. All night Alice lay awake in bed thinking about people pointing their fingers at her and talking about her behind her back.

The next day, Alice promised herself that she would try not to think about the cake and she would attend the fancy luncheon/bridal shower at the home of a friend and try to have a good time. Alice did not really want to attend because the hostess was a snob who more than once had looked down her nose at the fact that Alice was a single parent and not from the founding families of Tuscaloosa, but having already RSVP'd she could not think of a believable excuse to stay at home. The meal was elegant, the company was definitely upper crust old south and to Alice's horror, the CAKE in question was presented as dessert.

Alice felt the blood drain from her body when she saw the cake, she started out of her chair to rush to tell her hostess all about it, but before she could get to her feet, the Mayor's wife said, "What a beautiful cake!" Alice, who was still stunned, sat back in her chair when she heard the hostess, who was a prominent church member, say, "Thank you, I baked it myself."

Alice smiled and thought to herself, "GOD is good."

A Christmas to Remember

This is a real story…

Pa never had such compassion for the lazy or those who squandered their means and then never had enough for the necessities. But for those who were genuinely in need, his heart was as big as all outdoors. It was from that I learned the greatest joy in life comes from giving, not from receiving.

It was Christmas Eve 1881. I was fifteen years old and feeling like the world had caved in on me because there just hadn't been enough money to buy me the rifle I'd wanted for Christmas. We did the chores early that night for some reason. I just figured Pa wanted a little extra time so we could read in the Bible.

After supper was over, I took my boots off and stretched out in front of the fireplace and waited for Pa to get down the old Bible. I was still feeling sorry for myself, and to be honest, I wasn't in much of a mood to read Scriptures. But Pa didn't get the Bible. Instead he bundled up again and went outside. I couldn't figure it out because we had already done all the chores. I didn't worry about it long though; I was too busy wallowing in self-pity.

Soon Pa came back in. It was a cold, clear night out and there was ice in his beard. "Come on, Matt," he said. "Bundle up good, it's cold out tonight," I was really upset then. Not only wasn't I getting the rifle for Christmas, now Pa was dragging me out in the cold and for no earthly reason that I could see. We'd already done all the chores, and I couldn't think of anything else that needed doing, especially not on a night like this, but I knew Pa was not very patient at one dragging one's feet when he'd told them to do something, so I got up and put my boots back on and got my cap, coat, and mittens. Ma gave me a mysterious smile as I opened the door to leave the house. Something was up, but I didn't know what. Outside, I became even more dismayed. There in front of the house was a work team, already hitched to the big sled. Whatever it was we were going to do wasn't going to be a short, quick, little job. I could tell. We never hitched up this sled unless we were going to haul a big load.

Pa was already up on the seat, reins in hand. I reluctantly climbed up beside him. The cold was already biting at me. I wasn't happy. When I was on, Pa pulled the sled around the house and stopped in front of the woodshed. He got off and I followed. "I think we'll put on the high sideboards," he said. "Here, help me." The high sideboards! It had been a bigger job then I wanted to do with just the low sideboards on, but whatever it was we were going to do would be a lot bigger with the high sideboards on.

After we exchanged the sideboards, Pa went into the woodshed and came out with an armload of wood—the wood I'd spent all summer hauling down from the mountain, and then all fall sawing into blocks and splitting.

What was he doing? Finally I said something, "Pa," I asked, "what are you doing?"

"You been by the Widow Jenson's lately?" he asked. The widow Jenson lived about two miles down the road. Her husband had died year or so before and left her with three children, the oldest being eight.

Sure I'd been by, but so what? "Yeah," I said, "Why?"

"I rode by just today," Pa said. "Little Jakey was out digging around in the woodpile trying to find a few chips. They're out of wood, Matt." That was all he said and then he turned and went back into the woodshed for another armload of wood. I followed him. We loaded the sled so high that I began to wonder if the horses would be able to pull it.

Finally, Pa called a halt to our loading, then we went to the smoke house and Pa took down a big ham and a side of bacon. He handed them to me and told me to put them in the sled and wait. When he returned he was carrying a sack of flour over his right shoulder and a smaller sack of something in his left hand. "What's in the little sack?" I asked. "Shoes, they're out of shoes. Little Jakey just had gunnysacks wrapped around his feet when he was out in the woodpile this morning. I got the children a little candy too. It just wouldn't be Christmas without a little candy.

We rode the two miles to Widow Jenson's pretty much in silence. I tried to think through what Pa was doing. We didn't have much by worldly standards. Of course we did have a big woodpile, though most of what was left now was still in the form of logs that I would have to saw into blocks and split before we could use it. We also had meat and flour, so we could spare that, but I knew we didn't have any money, so why was Pa buying shoes and candy.

Really, why was he doing any of this? Widow Jenson had closer neighbors than us; it shouldn't have been our concern. We came in from the blind side of the Jenson house and unloaded the wood as quietly as possible, and then we took the meat and flour and shoes to the door. We knocked. The door opened a crack and a timid voice said, "Who is it?" "Lucas Miles, Ma'am, and my son, Matt. Could we come in for a bit?"

Widow Jenson opened the door and let us in. She had a blanket wrapped around her shoulders. The children were wrapped in another sitting in front of the fireplace by a very small fire that hardly gave off any heat at all. Widow Jenson fumbled with a match and finally lit the lamp. “We brought you a few things, Ma’am,” Pa said and sat down the sack of flour. I put the meat on the table. Then Pa handed her the sack that had the shoes in it.

She opened it hesitantly and took the shoes out one pair at a time. There was a pair for her and one for each of the children—sturdy shoes, the best, shoes that would last. I watched her carefully. She bit her lower lip to keep it from trembling and then tears filled her eyes and started running down her cheeks. She looked up at Pa like she wanted to say something, but it wouldn’t come out. “We brought a load of wood, too, Ma’am,” Pa said. He turned to me and said, “Matt, go bring in enough to last awhile. Let’s get that fire up to size and heat this place up.” I wasn’t the same person when I went back out to bring in the wood. I had a big lump in my throat and as much as I hate to admit it, there were tears in my eyes, too. In my mind I kept seeing those three kids huddled around the fireplace and their mother standing there with tears running down her cheeks with so much gratitude in her heart that she couldn’t speak. My heart swelled within me and joy that I’d never known before filled my soul. I had given at Christmas many times before, but never when it had made so much difference. I could see we were literally saving the lives of these people.

I soon had the fire blazing and everyone’s spirits soared. The kids started giggling when Pa handed them each a piece of candy and Widow Jenson looked on with a smile that probably hadn’t crossed her face for a long time. She finally turned to us, “God bless you,” she said. “I know the Lord has sent you. The children and I have been praying that he would send one of his angels to spare us.” In spite of myself, the lump returned to my throat and the tears welled up in my eyes again. I'd never thought of Pa in those exact terms before, but after Widow Jenson mentioned it I could see that it was probably true.

I was sure that a better man than Pa had never walked the Earth. I started remembering all the times he had gone out of his way for Ma and me, and many others. The list seemed endless as I thought on it. Pa insisted that everyone tried on the shoes before we left. I was amazed when they all fit and I wondered how he had known what sizes to get.

Then I guessed that if he was on an errand for the Lord that the Lord would make sure he got the right sizes. Tears were running down Widow Jenson's face again when we stood up to leave. Pa took each of the kids in his big arms and gave then a hug. They clung to him and didn't want us to go. I could see they missed their Pa, and I was glad that I still had mine.

At the door Pa turned to Widow Jenson and said, "The Mrs. wanted me to invite you and the children over for Christmas dinner tomorrow. The turkey will be more then the three of us can eat, and a man can get cantankerous if he has to eat turkey for too many meals. We'll be by to get you about eleven. It'll be nice to have some little ones around again. Matt, here, hasn't been little for quite a spell." I was the youngest. My two brothers and sisters had all married and had moved away. Widow Jenson nodded and said, "Thank you, Brother Miles. I don't have to say may the lord be with you. I know for certain that He will."

Out on the sled I felt a warmth that come from deep within and I didn't even notice the cold. When we had gone a ways, Pa turned to me and said, "Matt, I want you to know something. Your Ma and me have been tucking a little money away here and there all year so we could buy that rifle for you, but we didn't have quite enough. Then yesterday a man who owed me a little money from years back came by to make things square. Your ma and I were real excited, thinking that now we could get you that rifle, and I started into town this morning to do just that. But on the way I saw little Jakey out scratching in the woodpile with his feet wrapped in gunnysacks and I knew what I had to do. Son, I spent the money for shoes and a little candy for those children. I hope you understand."

I understood, and my eyes became wet with tears again. I understood very well, and I was so glad Pa had done it. Now the rifle seemed very low on my list of priorities. Pa had given me a lot more. He had given me the look on the Widow Jenson's face and the radiant smiles of her three children. For the rest of my life, whenever I saw any of the Jenson's, or split a block of wood, I remembered, and remembering brought back that same joy I felt riding home beside Pa that night. Pa had given me much more than a rifle that night, he had given me the best Christmas of my life.

Easter

Easter was always a fun time at our house. Mother would make new dresses for the girls and shirts for the boys, and games went on throughout the week. Each of the kids were given six eggs to hide and all through the week if you found someone else's eggs you were to re-hide the eggs. Then on Easter Sunday you had to find your six eggs. The winner of the contest had no chores for the following week.

Over the years the gift of hiding and imagination grew to become an art in the Ford house. Another thing that was enjoyed was waking up and getting dressed and running outside to find what the Easter Bunny had left you. The first one out got to choose their basket and so and so on. This one particular Easter Marie had decided she was going to be first up, dressed and outside. She had cleverly decided she was going to go to bed early. Ann and Sunshine knew what she had planned. She was fully dressed under her gown. She thought she would jump up in the morning throw the gown off and out the door.

For Marie stunts like this usually worked, but this time it slightly backfired.

Bright and early Easter morning she awoke, threw her gown off and started for the door. But before she could escape to the yard she was greeted by Mother. "I think since you slept in your clothes and they are all winkled, you should wait until last to get your basket," Mother said. Marie was so mad she thought someone had told on her, but Mother had started in the room when she saw Marie whip the gown over her head. But this incident was only a pause for Marie, she still remained very mischievous.

Putting Winning Aside: Don't Judge

What would you do? You make the choice! Don't look for a punch line, there isn't one. The question is: Would you have made the same choice?

At a fundraising dinner for a school that serves learning-disabled children, the father of one of the students delivered a speech that would never be forgotten by all who attended.

After extolling the school and its dedicated staff, he offered this question:

"When not interfered with by outside influences, everything nature does is done with perfection. Yet my son, Shay, cannot learn things as other children do. He cannot understand things as other children do. Where is the natural order of things in my son?"

The audience was stilled by the query. The father continued. "I believe that when a child like Shay, physically and mentally handicapped, comes into the world, an opportunity to realize true human nature presents itself, and it comes in the way other people treat that child." Then he told the following story:

Shay and his father had walked past a park where some boys Shay knew were playing baseball. Shay asked, "Do you think they'll let me play?"

Shay's father knew that most of the boys would not want someone like Shay on their team, but the father also understood that if his son were allowed to play, it would give him a much-needed sense of belonging and some confidence to be accepted by others in spite of his handicaps.

Shay's father approached one of the boys on the field and asked if Shay could play, not expecting much. The boy looked around for guidance and a few boys nodded in approval, why not? So he took matters into his own hands and said, "We're losing by six runs and the game is in the eighth inning. I guess he can be on our team; we'll try to put him in to bat in the ninth inning."

Shay struggled over to the team's bench, put on a team shirt with a broad smile and his father had a small tear in his eye and warmth in his heart. The boys saw the father's joy at his son being accepted.

In the bottom of the eighth inning, Shay's team scored a few runs but was still behind by three. In the top of the ninth inning, Shay put on a glove and played in right field. Even though no hits came his way, he was obviously ecstatic just to be in the fame and on the field, grinning from ear to ear as his father waved to him from the stands.

In the bottom of the ninth inning, Shay's team scored again, now, with two outs and bases loaded, the potential winning run was on base and Shay was scheduled to be next at bat.

At this juncture, do they let Shay bat and give away their chance to win the game?

Surprisingly, Shay was given the bat. Everyone knew that a hit was all but impossible because Shay didn't even know how to hold the bat properly, much less connect with the ball. However, as Shay stepped up to the plate, the pitcher, recognizing the other team putting winning aside for this moment in Shay's life, moved in a few steps to lob the ball in softly so Shay could at least be able to contact.

The first pitch came and Shay swung clumsily and missed. The pitcher again took a few steps forward to toss the ball softly towards Shay. As the pitch came in, Shay swung at the ball and hit a slow ground ball right back to the pitcher.

The game would now be over, but the pitcher picked up the soft grounder and could have easily thrown the ball to the first baseman. Shay would have been out and that would have been the end of the game. Instead, the pitcher threw the ball right over the head of the first baseman, out of reach of all the teammates. Everyone from the stands and both teams started yelling, "Shay, run to first! Run to first!" Never in his life had Shay ever ran that far but he made it to first base.

He scampered down the baseline, wide-eyed and startled. Everyone yelled, "Run to second, run to second!" Catching his breath, Shay awkwardly ran towards second gleaming and struggling to make it to second base.

By the time Shay started towards second base, the right fielder had the ball, the smallest guy on their team, who had a chance to be the hero for his team for the first time. He could have thrown the ball to the second-baseman for the tag, but he understood the pitcher's intentions, and he too, intentionally threw the ball high and far over the third baseman's head.

Shay ran toward second base deliriously as the runners ahead of him circled the bases toward home. All were screaming, "Shay, Shay, Shay, all the way Shay."

As Shay reached second base the opposing shortstop ran to help him and turned him in the direction of third base. Shouting, "Run to third! Shay, ran to third."

As Shay rounded third, the boys from both teams and those watching were on their feet, screaming, "Shay, run home!"

Shay ran to home, stepped on the plate, and was cheered as the hero who hit the "grand slam" and won the game for his team.

"That day," said the father softly, with tears rolling down his face, "the boys from both teams helped bring a piece of true love and humanity into this world."

Shay didn't make it to another summer and died that winter, having never forgotten being the hero making his father so happy, and coming home and seeing his mother tearfully embrace her little hero of the day!

Movie with David

It was a Friday night and my brother had taken my little sister and me to the show. We were so happy to get to go to the show and to go out and eat because this was a special treat. Really what it was he had to do was baby sit while Mother and Daddy were gone.

I remember that show so vividly because it made me think about death and the future. The movie was premature burial. The plot was about a man that thought and dreamed of being buried alive. So he made plans to be buried where if he were alive he could survive in the mausoleum he had bought for his burial plot. I remember that even though he had taken great care that if he was buried alive in the mausoleum that he could survive, but even the best of places he still failed.

That night when we went home the house was locked and we had to climb through the kitchen window. Guess who was chosen to enter the dark room? I shut my eyes and prayed as my brother pushed me through the tiny window into the kitchen sink. Next I had to climb down from the sink and find my way to the door. As I slowly walked to the door, trying to feel my way, I felt something touch my hand, all I could think of was that the man in that grave had managed to get in the house and he was going to grab me. So, I ran and managed to go to the door and let my brother and sister. When he turned on the light I discovered who had touched my hand it was Lady, my father's dog. I think that was the last time I had ever went to see a scary movie. I also decided that when I died I would be cremated, because I wanted to be sure I was dead. That was a fear that I did not want. That night I don't think I slept for a second. That was also the last time I went to the show with that brother.

Sometimes fears and death makes us stop and think about life. Each life touches the lives of others.

On "It's a Wonderful Life," George Bailey had a chance to see what life would be like if he did not exist. He discovered with the help of Clarence, the angel, that if it had not been for him the life of so many that he touched would be changed and people were better off for meeting him. In the end he feels those he helped along the way were there for him when he needed help.

In the end his brother tells him he is the richest man in town because of his friend, and like the angel Clarence inscribed in George's copy of *Tom Sawyer*,

"No man is a failure who has friends."

Friends

One day when I was a freshman in high school, I saw a kid from my class walking home from school. His name was Kyle. It looked like he was carrying all of his books. I thought to myself, "Why would anyone bring home all of his books on Friday? He must really be a nerd." I had quite a weekend planned, parties, and a football game with my friend's tomorrow afternoon, so I shrugged my shoulders and went on.

As I was walking, I saw a bunch of kids running toward him. They ran at him, knocking all his books out of his arms and tripping him so he landed in the dirt. His glasses went flying, and I saw him land in the grass about ten feet away from him. He looked up and I saw this terrible sadness in his eyes. My heart went out to him. So, I jogged over to him and as he crawled around looking for his glasses, I saw a tear in his eye.

As I handed him his glasses, I said, "Those guys are jerks. They really should get lives."

He looked at me and said, "Hey thanks!" There was a big smile on his face. It was one of those smiles that showed real gratitude. I helped him pick up his books, and asked him where he lived. As it turned out, he lived near me, so I asked him why I have never seen him before.

He said he had gone to a private school before now. I would

have never hung out with a private school kid before. We talked all the way home, and I carried his books. He turned out to be a pretty cool kid.

I asked him if he wanted to play football on Saturday with me and my friends.

He said yes. We hung out together all weekend and the more I got to know Kyle the more I liked him. And my friends thought the same of him. Monday morning came, and there was Kyle with the huge stack of books again.

I stopped him and said, "Boy, you are gonna really build some serious muscles with this pile of books everyday!"

He just laughed and handed me half the books.

Over the next four years, Kyle and I became best friends. When we were seniors, we began to think about college. Kyle decided on Georgetown and I was going to Duke. I knew that we would always be friends, and that the miles would never be a problem. He was going to be a doctor, and I was going on a football scholarship.

Kyle was valedictorian of our class. I teased him all the time about being a nerd. He had to prepare a speech for graduation. I was so glad it wasn't me having to get up there and speak.

Graduation day, I saw Kyle. He looked great. He was one of those guys that really found himself during high school. He filled out and actually looked good in glasses. He had more dates that made me and all the girls love him! Boy, sometimes I was jealous.

Today was one of those days. I could see that he was nervous about his speech. So, I smacked him on the back and said, "Hey, big guy, you'll be great!"

He looked at me with one of those looks, the really grateful ones, and smiled. "Thanks," he said. As he started his speech, he cleared his throat, and began. "Graduation is a time to thank those who helped you make it through those tough years. Your parents, your teachers, your siblings, maybe a coach… but mostly a friend to someone is the best gift you can give them. I am going to tell you a story."

I heard the gasp go through the crowd as this handsome, popular boy told us all about his weakest moment. I saw his Mom and Dad looking at me and smiling that same grateful smile. Not until that moment did I realize its depth.

Never underestimate the power of your actions. With one small gesture you can change a person's life. For better or for worse, God put us all in each other's lives to impact one another in some way. Look for good in others.

Journey Called Life

Quite a big message in this little mouse story… A mouse looked through the crack in the wall to see the farmer and his wife open a package. "What food might this contain?" The mouse wandered—he was devastated to discover it was a mousetrap.

Retreating to the farmyard, the mouse proclaimed the warning: "There is a mousetrap in the house! There is a mousetrap in the house!"

The chicken clucked and scratched, raised her head and said, "Mr. Mouse, I can tell this is a grave concern to you, but it is of no consequence to me. I cannot be bothered by it."

The mouse turned to the pig and told him, "There is a mousetrap in the house! There is a mousetrap in the house!"

The pig sympathized, but said, "I am so very sorry, Mr. Mouse, but there is nothing I can do about it but pray. Be assured you are in my prayers."

The mouse turned to the cow and said, "There is a mousetrap in the house! There is a mousetrap in the house!"

The cow said, "Wow, Mr. Mouse I'm sorry for you, but it is no skin off my nose."

So the mouse returned to the house, head down and subjected to face the farmer's mousetrap alone. That very night a sound was heard throughout the house—like the sound of a mouse-trap catching its prey. The Farmer's wife rushed to see what was caught. In the darkness, she did not see it was a venomous snake whose tail the trap had caught. The snake bit the farmer's wife. The farmer rushed her to the hospital, and she returned home with a fever. Everyone knows you treat a fever with fresh chicken soup, so the farmer took his hatchet to the farmyard for the soup's main ingredient. But his wife's sickness continued, so friend and neighbors came to sit with her around the clock. To feed them, the farmer butchered the pig. The farmer's wife did not get well; she died. So many people came for her funeral; the farmer had the cow slaughtered to provide enough meat for all of them.

The mouse looked upon it all from his crack in the wall with great sadness. So, the next time you hear someone is facing a problem and think it doesn't concern you, remember when one of us is threatened we are all at risk. We are all involved in this journey called life. We must keep an eye out for one another and make an extra effort to encourage one another. One of the best things to hold onto in this world is a friend.

Winter of '77

The winter of '77 was an adventure I will never forget. It was near the end of February and the beginning of a snow blizzard. Some people thought, "Yes, school is out and we can stay in and warm ourselves by the heater and sip hot chocolate." But for me it was fear I was well past due and just waiting for the labor pains and the birth of my fourth child. The snow covered the ground and became deeper and deeper, when finally I knew we were snowed in.

It seemed like the snow would never stop. Well it happened, we were snowed in and the pains began. There were only two families and one man, Crazy John, over the hill in the country where we lived. I called the doctor and he asked if anyone knew how to deliver a baby. Terry and I said no, but they guessed they could try. Crazy John said yes he could he talked to the doctor and said, "Yes, I've delivered calves. I just put a chain on them and pull it out." After hearing those words I asked to speak to the doctor one more time.

The doc and I agreed, John helping in the birth of my child might not be a good idea. The doctor and I spoke about what I could do until the baby was born or until we could get to the hospital.

It was a very long night but I was very lucky, a few hours later an emergency vehicle made it to the hospital before my daughter was born. We named her Charity because of God's love, and I was able to make it to the hospital before she was born.

Something to Think About

This is a commencement speech made by Anna Quindlen at Villanova:

It's a great honor for me to be the third member of my family to receive an honorary doctorate from this great university. It's an honor to follow my great uncle Jim, who was a gifted physician, and my uncle Jack, who is a remarkable businessman. Both of them could have told you something important about their professions, about medicine or commerce.

I have no specialized field of interest or expertise, which puts me at a disadvantage talking to you today. I'm a novelist. My work is human nature. Real life is all I know. Don't ever confuse the two, your life and your work. The second is only part of the first. Don't ever forget what a friend once wrote Senator Paul Tsongas when the senator decided not to run for re-election because he had been diagnosed with cancer. "No man ever said on his deathbed, I wish I had spent more time at the office."

Don't ever forget the words my father sent me on a postcard last year, "If you win the rat race, you're still a rat."

Or what John Lennon wrote before he was gunned down in the driveway of the Dakota: "Life is what happens while you're busy making other plans."

You will walk out of here this afternoon with only one thing that no one else has. There will be hundreds of people out there with your same degree; there will be thousands of people doing what you want to do for a living. But you will be the only person alive who has sole custody of your life. Your particular life. Your entire life. Not just your bank account, but your soul.

People don't talk about the soul very much anymore. It's so much easier to write a resume than to craft a spirit. But a resume is a cold comfort on a winter night, or when you're sad, or broke, or lonely, or when you've gotten back the test results and they're not so good.

Here is my resume:

I am a good mother to three children. I have tried never to let my profession stand in the way of being a good parent. I no longer consider myself center of the universe. I show up. I listen. I try to laugh. I am a good friend to my husband. I have tried to make marriage vows mean what they say. I am a good friend to my friends, and they to me. Without them, there would be nothing to say to you today, because I would be a cardboard cutout. But I call them on the phone, and I meet them for lunch.

I would be rotten or at best mediocre at my job, if those other things were not true. You cannot be really first rate at your work if your work is all you are.

So here is what I wanted to tell you today: Get a life. A real life, not a manic pursuit of the next promotion, the bigger paycheck, the larger house. Do you think you'd care so very much about those things if you blew an aneurysm one afternoon, or found a lump in your breast?

Get a life in which you notice the smell of salt water punish itself on a breeze over Seaside Heights, a life in which you stop and watch how a red tailed hawk circles over the water or the way a baby scowls with concentration when she tries to pick up a Cheerios with her thump and first finger.

Get a life in which you are not alone. Find people you love, and who love you. And remember that love is not leisure, it is work. Pick up the phone. Send an e-mail. Write a letter. Get a life in which you are generous. And realize that life is the best thing ever, and that you have no business taking it for granted. Care so deeply about its goodness that you want to spread it around.

Take money you would have spent on beers and give it to charity. Work in a soup kitchen. Be a big brother or sister. All of you want to do well. But if you do not do well too, then doing well will never be enough. It is so easy to waste our lives, our days, our hours, and our minutes. It is so easy to exist instead of to live.

I learned to live many years ago. Something really, really bad happened to me, something that changed my life in ways that, if I had my druthers, it would never have been changed at all. And what I learned from it is what, today, seems to be the hardest lesson of all. I learned to love the journey, not the destination. I learned that it is not a dress rehearsal, and that today is the only guaranteed you get. I learned to look at all the good in the world and try to give some of it back because I believed in it, completely and utterly. And I tried to do that in part by telling others what I had learned. By telling them this: Consider the lilies of the field. Look at the fuzz on the baby's ear. Read in the backyard with the sun on your face.

Learn to be happy. And think of life as a terminal illness, because if you do, you will live it with joy and passion as it ought to be lived.

Should Do List

Too many people put off something that brings them joy just because they haven't thought about it don't have it on their schedule, didn't know it was coming or are too rigid to depart from their routine.

I got to thinking one day about all those women on the Titanic who passed up dessert at dinner that fateful night in an effort to cut back. From then on, I've tried to be a little more flexible.

How many women out there will eat at home because their husband didn't suggest going out to dinner until after something had been thawed? Does the word "refrigeration" mean nothing to you?

How often have your kids dropped in to talk and sat in silence while you watched "Jeopardy" on television?

I cannot count the times I called my sister and said, "How about going to lunch in a half hour?" She would gas up and stammer, "I can't, I have clothes on the line. My hair is dirty. I wish I had known yesterday. I had a late breakfast. It looks like rain." And my personal favorite: "It's Monday." She died a few years ago. We never did have lunch together.

Because Americans cram so much into their lives, we tend to schedule our headaches. We live on a sparse diet of promises we make to ourselves when all the conditions are perfect!

We'll go back and visit the grandparents when we get Steve toilet-trained. We'll entertain when we replace the living room carpet. We'll go on a second honeymoon when we get two more kids out of college.

Life has a way of accelerating as we get older. The days get shorter, and the list of promises to us gets longer. One morning when we awaken and all we have to show for our lives is a list of, "I'm going to," "I plan on," and, "Someday, when things settle down a bit."

When anyone calls my 'seize the moment' friend, she is open to adventure and available for trips. She keeps an open mind on new ideas. Her enthusiasm for life is contagious. You talk with her for five minutes, and you're ready to trade your bad feet for a pair of Rollerblades and skip an elevator for a bungee cord.

My lips have not touched ice cream in ten years. I love ice cream. It's just that I might as well apply it directly to my stomach with a spatula and eliminate the digestive process. The other day, I stopped the car and bought a triple-decker (ice cream cone). If my car had hit an iceberg on my way home I would have died happy.

Now…go on and have a nice day. Do something you want to…not something on your should do list. If you were going to die soon and had only one phone call you could make, whom would you call and what would you say? And why are you waiting?

Have you ever watched kids playing on a merry go round or listened to the rain lapping on the ground? Ever followed a butterfly's erratic flight or gazed at the sun into the fading night? Do you run through each day on the fly? When you ask, how are you?" Do you hear the reply?

When the day is done, do you lie in your bed with the next hundred chores running through your head? Have you ever told your child, "We'll do it tomorrow," and in your haste not see his sorrow? Ever lost touch? Let a good friendship die? Just called you to say, "Hi."

When you worry and hurry though your day, it is like an unopened gift…. Thrown away…Life is not a race. Take it slower. Hear the music before the song is over.

A Story to Live By

My brother-in-law opened the bottom drawer of my sister's bureau and lifted out a tissue-wrapped-package. "This," he said, "is not a slip. This is lingerie."

He discarded the tissue and handed me the slip. It was exquisite silk, handmade and trimmed with a cobweb of lace. The price tag, with an astronomical figure on it, was still attached. "Jan bought this the first time we went to New York, at least eight or nine years ago. She never wore it. She was saving it for a special occasion. Well, I guess this is the occasion." He took the slip from me and put it on the bed with the other clothes we were taking to the mortician.

His hands lingered on the soft material for a moment, and then he slammed the drawer shut and turned to me. "Don't ever save anything for a special occasion. Everyday you're alive is a special occasion."

I remembered those words through the funeral and the days that followed when I helped him and my niece attend to all the sad chores that follow an unexpected death. I thought about them on the plane returning to California from the Midwestern town where my sister's family lives. I thought about all the things that she hadn't seen or heard or done. I thought about the things she had done without realizing that they were special. I'm still thinking about his words, and they've changed my life.

I'm reading more and dusting less. I'm sitting on the deck and admiring the view without fussing about the weeds in the garden. I'm spending more time with my family and friends and less time in committee meetings. Whenever possible, life should be a pattern of experience to savor, not endure.

I'm trying to recognize these moments now and cherish them. I'm not "saving" anything; we use our good china and crystal for every special event-such losing a pound, getting the sink unstopped, the first camellia blossom. I wear my good blazer to the market if I feel like it. My theory is if I look prosperous, I can shell out $28.49 for one small bag of groceries without wincing. I'm not saving my good perfume for special parties; clerks in hardware stores and tellers in banks have noses that function as well as my party-going friends.

"Someday" and "one of these days" are losing their grip in my vocabulary. If it's worth seeing or hearing or doing, I want to see, hear, and do it now. I'm not sure what my sister would've done had she known she wouldn't be here tomorrow; we all take for granted. I think she would have called family members and a few close friends. She might have called a few former friends to apologize and mend fences for past squabbles. I like to think she would have gone out for Chinese dinner, her favorite food. I'm guessing- I'll never know. It's those little things left undone that would make me angry if I knew that my hours were limited. Angry because I put off seeing good friends whom I was going to get in touch with—someday. Angry because I hadn't written certain letters that I intended to write—one of these days. Angry and sorry that I didn't tell my husband and daughter often enough how much I truly love them.

I'm trying very hard not to put off, hold back, or save anything that would add laughter and luster to our lives. And every morning when I open my eyes, I tell myself that it is special. Every day, every minute, every breath truly is… a gift from God.

Ballerina

I don't know how much time I have left. I've spent my life dispensing salves and purgatives, potions and incantations—miracles of nature, though I admit that some were pure medicine-show snake oil. Actually, half of the time all I offered was just plain common sense. Over the years, every kind of suffering person had made his or her way here. Some had broken limbs, or broken bodies...or hearts. Often their sorrow was an ailing son or daughter. It was always so hard when they'd lose a child. I never did get used to that. And then there were the young lovers. Obtaining their heart's desire was so important to them. I had to smile. I always made sweat and beg for their handful of bark, and for those willful tortures I'll probably go to hell… if there is one. My God, how long had it been since I had those feelings myself? The fever, the lump in my throat, the yearning. I can't remember. A long time…maybe never. Well, there have been other passions for me. There's my dusty legion of jars, each one hold its little secret. Barks, roots, soils, leaves, flowers, mushrooms, bugs—magic dust, every bit of it. There's my book—my "rudder", a ship's pilot would call it. That's a good name for it. Every salve, every purgative… they're all in there, everything that is, except my stained beard, scraggly hair, and flowing robes—they'll have to figure those out on their own.

And then there's my walking stick, always faithful…and the ballerina. And ten thousand mornings, ten thousand afternoons, ten thousand nights. And the stars. Oh, I have had my loves.

It hurts to move. My shelf and jars seem so far away, though I know that if I tried I could reach them. But no. It's enough and it's time…almost. I hope he make's it back in time. He bursts though my door only two days ago, a young man, well spoken. Tears were streaming down his face. He looked so bent and broken that I could not refuse him. He told me that his wife had died over a month ago and that he had been miserable since. "Please help me," he pleaded, "or kill me" He covered his face with his hands. "Perhaps they are the same thing. I don't know anymore."

I let him cry awhile so I could watch him, gauge him. When at last he looked up, with my good hand I motioned him to take a seat. Then, between sobbing fits, I went to work. "Do you see that toy there?" I said. "The little ballerina…Yes, that's it. Pick it up."

"Pick it up?"

"It won't bite. Pick it up." (He probably thought it was a trick—that's what they expect.) He grasped it carefully, with one hand, and then wiped his eyes with the other. "That's better," I continued. "That's just a toy to you. You don't know what meaning to put to it, yet. So I want you to look at that ballerina."

He was hesitant, but I waited stubbornly, until he looked down and fixed his attention on the little toy dancer, I went on: "I knew a young man once who was very handsome—always had been. He not only turned every head, he was strong and smart, and his family was wealthy. His main concern each day was which girl he should court that evening. He had planned that after several season of playing at love he would marry a beautiful girl, have beautiful children, and settle down to spend thc money his father had promised him. And he had plans for that money. He had already purchased the land he wanted to live on and was having built there the biggest house in the area. He was going to raise and racehorses, I think. One morning he got on his favorite horse and went for a ride. He whipped that house into a gallop; it stepped in a hole and threw him. The young man broke his neck, and died." I stared at my guest and waited.

"That's a tragedy," he finally croaked.

"For whom? For those he left behind, perhaps. But was it for him? When he opened his eyes that morning, he didn't know he would die that day. He had no intention of dying for another sixty years—if then. None of us do." The young man looked confused. "His mistake was that he forgot that he could die that day."

"That's a morbid thought," he replied, and he looked as though he had just smelled something putrid.

"Is it? A moment ago you asked me to end your grieving by ending your own life. Suppose I oblige?" I stared at him for a few moments with my most practiced penetrating glare. "Suppose I did agree to kill you. How would you spend your last few minutes?"

He was still a little wary of me, but relieved that I seemed to be suggesting a hypothetical situation, rather than a serious course of action. He considered the possibilities for a while, and then straightened in his chair. "Well, I guess I would stop outside and take a last, best look at the sky, the clouds, and the trees."

"Suppose you lived that way all the time?" He stared at me, then looked down at his hands, searching them. "That young man I told you about…perhaps the tragedy for him was not that he died, but that he failed to use the eventual certainty of his death to make him live! Did he woo each of those ladies as though it might be his last romance? Did he build that house as though it might be his last creation? Did he ride that horse as though it would be his last ride? I don't know; I hope so." My young guest nodded, but he was still sad. I pointed to the toy ballerina he was holding. "That was given to me by a young lady who understood these things,"

He looked at it closely, "Is she a dancer?"

"Yes she is, and she is dead." The young man looked up, once again off balance. "She has been dead for, oh, a very long time." After all these years, a tear fell down my cheek. I let it go. "She was many things. A child, a woman, a cook and a gardener, a friend, a lover, a daughter…. But what she really was—who she was—was a dancer. When she was dying, she gave that doll to me, smiled, and whispered, 'At the moment of my death, I will take all of my dancing and put it in there so my dancing can live on.'"

Tears welled in my guest's eyes.

"I can help you," I said, "but first there is something that you must do." He became very attentive. "Go to town and knock on the door of the first house you come to. Ask the people inside if their family has ever been touched by death. If so, go in the next house. When you find a family that has not been touched by death, bring them to me. Do you understand?" He nodded, and I sighed. "I'm tired now."

He got up, set the ballerina back on the table, and started for the door. I stopped him, "Young man!" He faced me from the doorway. "Come back as soon as you can."

It's late. I wonder what Death will look like? A drooling ogre? Perhaps an unblinking skull, the Grim Reaper? A veiled mistress with beckoning arms? The standard forms. Or maybe Death will be a polished young man in a three-piece suit, all smiles and sincerity and confidence. What a disappointment that would be. No, I prefer the scythe—no ambiguity, no surrender… no dickering. What's that I hear him? He's here.

"May I come in?"

I nod. It's the young man who left me two days ago to knock on the doors of his neighbors' homes. "Well…?" My breath is shorter than I thought.

He smiles, looks down at his hands, then back at me. "Well, I did as you said. It didn't take long before I realized that I wasn't going to find a household that hadn't been touched by death.

"How many did you go to?"

He covers his mouth with his hand a moment, trying to hide his pride, I guess.

"All of them."

"All?"

"Every house…I'm very stubborn."

We both smile. My wheezing is worse, and he notices. He shows his concern, and I see that he understands what is happening.

"You're dying aren't you, old man?"

I close my eyes in answer. When I open them again he is at my side.

"Is there someone I should get for you? Your family?"

"Gone."

"Some friends?"

"Gone. All gone…except for you." The young man nods, and then pulls a chair over next to my own. He takes my hand. I rest a moment. "There is something you must do for me," I wheeze. "When I'm dead burn this house and everything in it, including me."

"Leave nothing behind?"

"This is only a filthy old shack. I'm leaving behinds the only thing that anyone really can leave behind… the difference I've made in the lives of the people I've met." I squeeze his hand as best I can. He squeezes back. "Oh… and this." I try to lift the book in my lap—my book. He sees me struggling and picks it up for me. "You take this. It's yours." His eyes widen.

"But I don't deserve—"

"There isn't time for that now!" He nods and puts the book on his lap. Good, that's done. Moments pass. It gets quieter…I close my eyes. I think again the glory of ten thousand mornings, then thousand afternoons, ten thousand nights… then they too fade. All that's left is the sound of our breathing and the wind. Time slows. Time changes. Where are the scythes? The young man's hand leaves mine and I hear his footsteps reside… stop… return…. He sits down and I feel his hand on mine. He opens my fingers and lay something cool and light in my palm all lace and limbs… the ballerina.

Now I can go.

I Wonder Why

Another bad night filled with dreams I could not put the pieces of the dreams together, but I knew something was about to happen. I started having dreams again in October of 1979, but when I woke up, I could not remember the dream but only bits and pieces. This continued until December.

In November I had a dream I didn't remember. I was so scared in the dream I remember my ten-year-old son and my seven-year-old son were in a bad car wreck and hurt seriously. I woke before I knew what had happened to them. I was so scared that I went and checked on them to be sure they were ok. Within a few days I had another dream of them being taken to the hospital ER, and one had died. I woke again and began praying, "Lord, please don't take my sons, take me instead." Each day I became more and more scared to go to sleep. Again a few nights passed and I had another dream. This time there was a bad wreck, but a few minutes before the wreck I say my youngest son getting in the front seat of our truck. The ten-year-old was in the front of the truck. The next moment in the dream I received a call to go to the hospital my ten-year-old son was seriously injured. An angel in the dream showed me a coffin with a young lady in the casket that looked a lot like me, but younger.

When I awoke again I was so scared but relieved that maybe God had heard my prayers and I was going to die instead of my sons. A short time later on December 12th my husband and children and I were on our way to my mother's house in Miner to stay because we were in the process of building our home and we were staying with her.

We had truck trouble and my mother came and got myself and my two girls to take home. The boys stayed with their dad and waited on our neighbors who were coming to help.

Little did I know the dream was starting to unfold.

Mother took us home and I was getting the girls ready for bed when the telephone began ringing. I went to answer the phone and the caller told me to come to the hospital; there had been a bad wreck. I went to the hospital and upon arriving my husband was with my youngest son. I for some reason was not as scared as I might have been because I started thinking about the dream and knew in my heart my sons' were not going to die. As my husband came towards me he told me Tony was badly injured but him and our neighbor were just bruised and my youngest son, he said, had just got into the front seat of the truck when the wreck happened.

My oldest son was soon transferred to a bigger hospital where he could be cared for.

When he arrived at the hospital, the doctors started working on him and running tests. His leg was broken seriously and he was losing blood. The next couple of days he was in ICU. He had blood transfusions and his leg was pinned together and placed elevated in traction. On the third day, he was doing better and my sisters came to stay with him so I could go home for a while. I was very reluctant because of the dream and this was the third day. I kissed my son bye and told him I would be back soon.

On my way home I began thinking about my other three children and the dream. When I made it to my mother's house, I was so tired. It was late and the kids were still awake waiting for me. After hugs, kisses, and stories they were soon in bed sound asleep. Later I went to sleep, totally exhausted. A short time later the phone began to ring. It was my brother calling to let me know my niece Laura Dawn had committed suicide and died at her home. She was married and expecting a baby. I was so shocked and could not believe what I heard. I had to let my mother know what had happened. That morning when mother was up I told her about Laura Dawn. Later that day we were told they were going to cremate her. I went back to the hospital to relieve my sisters who were staying with my son and to let them know about Laura Dawn.

Later when they had gone home I started thinking about the dream. That is when I realized the person in the coffin was not me it was Laura Dawn. She looked a lot like me but younger.

A few months later, I remembered I started writing a letter to Laura Dawn and wishing her a happy birthday, but I never finished the letter. It is still to this day in the typewriter. I still think, if only I had finished the letter and mailed it, maybe it would have made a difference. I'll never know.

This is why we should never put things off. Live as each day is your last and remember we can't go back.

The Journey's End

Each life touches the lives of others. In "It's A Wonderful Life," George Bailey had a chance to see what life would be like if he did not exist. He discovered with the help of Clarence the angel that if it had not been for him the lives of so many he touched would have changed and people were better off for meeting him. In the end when he feels as though everything is over, all those he helped along the way were there for him when he needed help.

In the end his brother tells him he is the richest man in town because of his friends, and Clarence tells him, "No man is a failure who has friends" (inscribed in a copy of *Tom Sawyer*).

So many people walk around with a meaningless life. They seem half-asleep, even when they are busy doing things they think are important. This is because they are chasing the wrong things. The way you get meaning into your life is to devote yourself to loving others, devote yourself to your community around you, and devote yourself to creating something that gives you purpose and meaning." The culture we have does not make people feel good about themselves, and you have to be strong enough to say if the culture doesn't work, don't buy it.

The most important thing in life is to learn to give out love, and let it come in. How useful it would be to put a daily limit on self-pity, just a few tearful minutes, then on with the day. Sometimes you cannot believe what you see you have to believe what you feel.

It would be nice if our lives were like movies on tape, where we could rewind and correct all our mistakes and change our destination and undo all things that we regret we did. But life is not that way.

There are so many things in life that we cannot do anything about, so why do we worry. The past is gone, the present is here, enjoy it because if you let things and people get you angry then you have let them win and you are robbed of time you could be happy. Life is like a rainbow, we never know when it will appear. It has many beautiful colors, the same as there are many beautiful people of all colors that blending and sharing of colors is what makes it so beautiful. The rainbow appears after the rains have cleansed the Earth, just as the beauty of the rainbow is seen in the faces of those who have made us laugh and shared their love and kindness with us. The feelings have cleansed our soul. The saying is that if you follow the end of the rainbow you will find a pot of gold. The pot of gold at the end of the rainbow is actually your treasures of memories and love that you have accumulated while traveling the path of life. And last but not least the rainbow is found in the sky and we have to look up to see all of its beauty. Life is the same way, to enjoy the beauty of life we have to look up and follow our dreams.

"What if" and "what only" will only stop you from going on. To make the journey and not fall in love then all is wasted. Try and try again. I want you to get swept away and I want you to laminate, sing like a bird, and dance like a ballerina. There is a time to sew and a time to weep, but remember nothing lasts. If you haven't tried you haven't lived. You make your choices. Take care of each other the best you can and be sorry for nothing. No one is going to bat 100% or even close to it. All that is important is that, generally speaking, you are doing your best and that you are moving in the right direction.

Life is a journey and we should enjoy the journey. Change is your friend and not your enemy. That's not to say change won't sometimes be scary and disconcerting, but it can be a lot less frightening if you understand that you do have the power over the outcome. What is the magical power? You and your attitude, a positive attitude gets positive results. Remember: no man is a failure who has friends and faith.

Remember, a bend in the road is not the end of the road, as long as you remember to make the turn. "See You Around The Corner."

About the Author

Shirley Coleman is a woman who knows what it is like to face hard times. A country girl born in Miner Switch, Missouri, and the eleventh child of twelve siblings, she has experienced many trials and tribulations throughout her life.

Shirley is a school counselor and teacher, preacher's wife, mother, grandmother, friend to many, and a fine Christian lady. Her purpose in writing this book is to provide the reader with strength, faith and encouragement to endure the trials of life, and to understand that since events of the past can't be changed, it is best to reflect on these events and apply the lessons learned for a better tomorrow.

Index